Praise for Refocusi

"A practical guide for the practitioner, a primer for the less experienced, and a useful reference for focus group veterans to remind us all how to fully lever the focus group tool. . . . a light to illuminate the dark back room and ensure the insights can shine through the shadows of the focus group process."

—Graham P. Milner, Executive Vice President,
Global Innovation, WD-40 Company

". . . a valuable gem. It brings high level theory in anthropology and psychology down to basics, translated into practical advice that a range of researchers can follow. The author writes from his extensive experience in marketing and advertising, with the anthropologist peeking through."

—Timothy de Waal Malefyt, Vice President, Director of
Cultural Discoveries, BBDO Worldwide

" . . . clearly and concisely lays out what should and shouldn't be done . . . demystifies the focus group and sets it in perspective. Highly readable and very informative. A must read for those who conduct focus groups, but more important for those who commission them and use the results."

—C. Samuel Craig, Catherine and Peter Kellner Professor,
Director, Entertainment Media and Technology Program,
and Deputy Chair, Marketing Department,
Stern School of Business, New York University

". . . an invaluable resource for marketers. For too long, focus groups have proceeded along with no one bothering to break them down the way this expert has. (Morais') insights into what makes a focus group tick, or 'should' make it tick, are dead-on. This book will provide clients and agencies alike with fresh eyes to view not only their consumers, but also what their products and services are truly offering."

—Alan Braunstein, Creative Director, Kaplan Thaler Group

"Thoughtful, funny, but most of all, helpful! In bringing experience and a keen observational eye to focus groups, Morais shows what continues to make face-to-face focus groups powerful tools and what undermines their ability to shed light. This volume is a reminder, candidly penned, of the need to pay attention. Required reading."

—Rita Denny and Patricia Sunderland, authors of
Doing Anthropology in Consumer Research

"At a time when too much is tested in focus groups and not enough learned, (Morais') training as an anthropologist gives rise to many good ideas (and reminders for experienced marketers) about how to gain an understanding of the consumer psyche that drives successful advertising."

—Jeff Shaffer, Managing Partner & Co-Founder,
Flywheel Accelerated Solutions

". . . refreshingly informative without being too preachy or didactic . . . a must read for anyone involved in qualitative research—from the client, agency, or research fields."

—Lisa Blumenstein, Strategic Planning Director,
Euro RSCG Worldwide

". . . an incisive, practical, and immensely readable account. . . . deftly guides us through potential disasters and pitfalls towards successful and useful results. *Refocusing Focus Groups* will without doubt enable practitioners to improve the quality of this indispensable research methodology."

—Brian Moeran, Professor of Business Anthropology,
Copenhagen Business School

Refocusing
Focus Groups

A Practical Guide

Robert J. Morais

Paramount Market Publishing, Inc.

Paramount Market Publishing, Inc.
950 Danby Road, Suite 136
Ithaca, NY 14850
www.paramountbooks.com
Telephone: 607-275-8100; 888-787-8100
Facsimile: 607-275-8101

Publisher: James Madden

Editorial Director: Doris Walsh

Cataloging in Publication Data available

ISBN-10: 0-9819869-7-8 | ISBN-13: 978-0-9819869-7-5

For Janie, Daniel, and Betsy

 # Contents

 **Preface**

THE IDEA for this book came to me on a flight back to the New York area from Chicago after three days of extremely difficult focus groups. On the first day, we exposed too many concepts, the moderator was not at her best, and the client grew irritated. I thought about what went wrong and how, and on the last day of the research, we made it right; the concept for a succinct, highly readable primer on best practices for focus groups began to take shape on a small sheet of paper on the tray table before me.

First, I thought of Strunk and White's *The Elements of Style,* as my guide. Then, the image of the most recent book I read, Michael Pollan's *Food Rules,* entered my mind. I concluded that my little book might appeal to busy marketing, marketing research, and advertising professionals who prefer not to wade through typical marketing research tomes, as well as to lay readers interested in consumer research. I thought that it would also be valuable to marketing professors and their students as a fast read on qualitative research techniques, a supplement to heavier course texts. I was excited about the prospect that a book like this one could help professionals avoid the kind of experience that inspired it. If that last objective is achieved, the events in Chicago will have been worth every stressful moment.

Introduction
The Use and Abuse of Focus Groups

IMAGINE you are attending a focus group. The viewing room is dimly lighted to ensure that the people being interviewed in the adjacent room do not see the observers peering through the one-way mirror. The spectators include several managers from a consumer packaged goods corporation: an assistant brand manager in his late 20s, a brand manager in her early 30s, a group marketing director in his late 30s, and an insight manager in her early 50s. Also present in this room (the "back room") is an advertising agency creative team consisting of an art director and copywriter, both in their late 30s, a mid-level ad agency account planner in her early 30s (responsible for crafting the creative brief, the blueprint for the brand's advertising), a junior ad agency account executive in her mid-20s, a mid-level ad agency account executive in her early 30s, and the principal of the marketing research firm that is conducting these focus groups, in his mid-50s.

The focus group moderator, in her late 40s, employed by the research company, and now seated inside the interview room, is engaged with five consumers or "respondents" as they are known in the industry. She is questioning them about household cleaning products. Later in the session she will solicit their reactions to television advertising storyboards pertaining to the manufacturer's cleaning brand.

Over the course of a day, the moderator will conduct four 90-minute focus groups. Between groups, there will be breaks for her and the observers to discuss new questions to be asked of the respondents. Between the second and third groups, there will be a one-hour pause for lunch, served in the observation room, during which the back room observers and the moderator will share personal thoughts on the findings of the research at halftime. A similar discussion, with closure and next steps specified, will occur after the last focus group of the day. Within a few days, the research firm will email the entire team a brief preliminary report of the findings called a Topline. The final report will be issued about two weeks after the sessions.

The moderator begins each focus group with a warm up. She introduces herself and explains that she does not work directly for the company that manufactures the brand. She makes it clear that she does not care if the respondents like or dislike what they will be shown; she wants their honest answers. She explains that observers are watching behind the mirror and that the sessions are being recorded. Then she asks each of the respondents, in this case, all women in their 30s through their 50s from Northern New Jersey, to briefly introduce themselves by name and share something about their lives, which invariably includes their marital status, number of children, and their occupation, if they work outside the home. All of this information is on sheets of paper available to the observers in the viewing room. The introductions are intended to relax the respondents before they begin the real work of the session: to reply to the questions in the "moderator's guide" that has been crafted by the research company with input from the marketing and advertising teams. Today's task is to learn which advertising language and graphics sell the brand most effectively and to winnow down the number of storyboards for planned quantitative testing.

Many of the observers—the assistant brand manager, the insight manager, the account planner, the copywriter, and the art director, foremost among them—take notes on the session, recording respondents' comments and keeping records of their stated purchase intent. On a scale of one through five, with one representing "Definitely Would Buy" and five representing "Definitely Would Not Buy," respondents declare their position after viewing each of four storyboards. The observers also record how well consumers comprehend the main idea of the advertising, whether the message is meaningful to them, what they like and dislike about the advertising language and graphics, and their rank ordering of the storyboards at the end of the session.

The account executive and senior level marketing managers take fewer notes, while the research company Principal jots down respondent comments that yield interesting findings or insights. Everyone observing focus groups is after "insights"—the in-vogue term in marketing—although on this particular day, the major concern is which of the storyboards is the most interesting and motivating to consumers. Even with this goal, the observers record flashes of personal insight ignited by the discussion in the interview room. As the focus groups advance, the observers share their thoughts with their colleagues in the back room. Their purpose is to "float" ideas and, not incidentally, impress their cohorts with their perceptiveness.

The observers sporadically conduct office work on their laptops, read emails, surf the web, check stock market updates or news, and engage in other activities as their attention to the interviews waxes and wanes. When their cell phones vibrate or ring, they dash out of the room to respond. Their concentration does not drift for long, and they return quickly from their calls. They do so because focus groups are often the primary means that marketers have to understand what and how their customers think. Focus groups are their opportunity to make contact, albeit separated by glass, with consumers whose willingness to exchange money for brands is the reason these professionals are employed.

SEVERAL years ago, two anthropologists who helped manufacturers learn about consumer behavior and beliefs in natural settings—homes, offices, and stores—argued in their company marketing materials that focus groups are an inferior method of consumer research. They wondered, "Why did it never occur to an anthropological fieldworker to sit his or her respondents around a table in the middle of their village, feed them a sandwich and a soda, then ask them to describe their lives, rituals, social hierarchy, and sense of kinship?" The reason: respondents often cannot report on their lives accurately or perceptively in such a situation. People live their lives, and certainly reflect upon them, but anthropologists and other social scientists use sophisticated techniques that enable them to understand people in ways respondents do not understand themselves.

Even with so many methodological options, from real-world based ethnographic observation to online chat rooms to complex surveys, marketers still field hundreds of thousands of focus groups annually. Advocates see them as a fast, inexpensive way to hear consumers speak about what they need and want, as well as a means to personally witness consumers' reactions to new product ideas, packaging innovations, and advertising concepts. At the same time, executives admit ruefully that they have allowed a few focus groups to determine a winning creative idea or predict the sales potential of a new product.

Jon Steel, in his book, *Truth, Lies & Advertising,* expresses the marketing and advertising industry's ambivalence about focus groups. At one point he says, "I believe that the thoughts and behavior of a human focus group respondent are as representative of the broader population as the thoughts and behavior of a chimpanzee in the San Francisco Zoo are of chimps in the East African forests. Which is to say, not very representative at all." Later in the book, he argues that only focus groups are suitable for obtaining consumer responses to advertising concepts and contends that interaction among focus group participants often brings insights that other research cannot. Even some anthropologists believe focus groups have merit, providing the interview content is not taken at face value. Patricia Sunderland and Rita Denny argue in their book, *Doing Anthropology in Consumer Research,* that the "talk" in focus groups is rich in meaning. When we attend closely to that meaning, much can be gained about consumer attitudes and sentiments.

I have witnessed thousands of focus groups and moderated many others. I am a champion of focus groups. At the same time, I am concerned about the selection of this research tool when another method would be superior. I worry when the wrong kinds of questions or too many questions, asked in machine gun fashion, mislead marketing and advertising agency executives. I fret that marketers, along with their ad agency partners, make ill-informed judgments and arrive at non-projectable conclusions that can damage their business.

Rather than allow my anxieties to lead me to end my association with focus groups, I decided to write this book. My aim is to lay out, in simple terms, the best practices for planning, designing, conducting, and interpreting focus groups. This book is not a substitute for in-depth volumes on focus groups. It is an adjunct to these treatments, one that should be referred to when focus groups are planned by marketers and their advertising agencies. My hope is that *Refocusing Focus Groups* will help focus group practitioners improve the quality of this indispensable research methodology.

Refocusing Focus Groups is divided into six parts:

Part 1: Before the Focus Group, Focus the Research
Part 2: Guide the Guide
Part 3: Listening and Observing
Part 4: Back Room Conduct
Part 5: Interpretation
Part 6: Conclusions and Resolutions

The sequence of this book reflects the order in which focus groups are planned and conducted. The chapters within each section can be read in order or not, however the practitioner feels that they are most useful.

Part 1

Before the Focus Group, Focus the Research

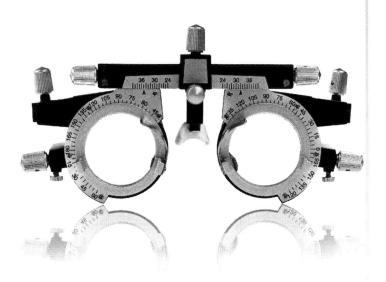

Why are we doing focus groups, anyway?

INSIGHT may be the most overused word in marketing research today. There are insight groups, insight managers, insight companies, and shopper insights—in addition to that rarity, insights themselves. When a word gains such currency, it is worthwhile to recall its formal definition to be sure that the meaning has not been compromised. An insight, defined by dictionary.com, entails ". . . apprehending the true nature of a thing, esp. through intuitive understanding: penetrating mental vision or discernment; faculty of seeing into inner character or underlying truth."

Focus groups are an ideal research choice for gaining insights. They allow for open-ended questions and expansive answers, and the process stimulates observation room conversations that can generate the "penetrating mental vision or discernment" that defines insights. Many manufacturers recognize the value in such discussions and field focus groups for deep understanding of their customers. Sometimes, though, focus groups are selected as a quick, low cost methodology to answer questions that are better included in quantitative research. Certainly, responses by 20 consumers to queries regarding how often and in what ways a brand is used cannot be projected to all consumers, and taking such findings to the bank can lead to financial losses. In addition, questions better deployed in a survey take precious time away from the probing that is the hallmark of qualitative studies.

Surveys are not the only alternative to focus groups. Observational research, sometimes called ethnography among marketing research professionals, in-depth one-on-one interviews, research on blogs and online chat rooms, and other methods also have a place in the marketing research toolbox. Several of these options will be discussed in this book.

2

How many respondents should we focus on?

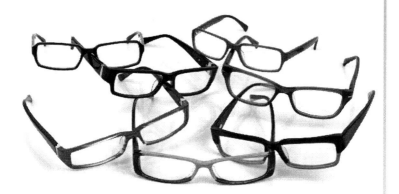

SOME marketers believe that the ideal number of consumers in a focus group is eight to ten. Their reasoning is that this group size will provide a variety of responses, and a full room is better than a half-full room. My experience is just the opposite. A smaller group of people, about five respondents, allows for more commentary from each person and a greater depth of discussion throughout the session. Fewer participants spawn less "groupthink," which is especially problematic when people are asked to react to innovative ideas. Another reason to keep the group small is that in larger groups a few of the respondents may feel comfortable remaining relatively silent. More intimate groups, with two or three people, can be highly effective, especially when responses to advertising are required.

Occasionally, the best option is to speak with one person at a time. One-on-one interviews should be chosen for particularly sensitive topics, such as finances or sex, or when personal retrospection or reflection can help inform a brand's strategy. You might decide to expose consumers individually to advertising in a focus group room to avoid the influence of other respondents on their perceptions. After all, aside from bars and airports, most people do not watch commercials with groups of strangers.

Know who you're inviting

A NUMBER of years ago, I was involved in observational research for a well-known floor cleaner. We pre-recruited women who were willing to have marketing and advertising types visit their homes and scrutinize them as they used our product. A problem arose when we asked our respondents to take out their brand (ours) from their kitchen cabinet. To our surprise, they removed a store brand version of our brand from their cupboard and referred to it without hesitation as our brand. Even after questioning, with the store brand right before their eyes, respondents used our brand name! We realized that, despite all our advertising, we had not done an adequate job of separating ourselves from knockoff competition. Our recruiting mistake, assuming that when consumers said they used *our* brand they meant *our* brand, led to valuable knowledge. Advertising and packaging needed to work harder to distinguish the brand. We resolved to have potential respondents read and describe the label of the brand in their cupboard when they were being recruited by telephone for future research projects.

4   Add segments, multiply groups

MANUFACTURERS often want to market their brand to more than one segment of consumers. When they do so, they must specify recruitment criteria that will ensure that the right group of respondents is asked the right questions, and they must conduct a sufficient number of focus groups.

The marketing goal may be to increase consumption of a pickle brand among current users, convert competitive pickle brand buyers to the marketer's brand, and/or convince non-pickle eaters to start eating pickles.

If the last two objectives are adopted, marketers must be sure that their loyal consumers are not disenfranchised when the brand is promoted to non-buyers. Additionally, the manufacturer may intend to market its pickles to different age, ethnic, income, or psychographic groups. Marketers must be cognizant of variations within these target segments. The broad descriptor, Asian American, represents Americans with Chinese, Japanese, Asian-Indian, Korean, Vietnamese, and Filipino heritages—among others. Some psychographic designations can also be misleading. Baby Boomers were born between 1946 and 1964. A Boomer born in 1950 was 19 during Woodstock and the Vietnam War protests. A Boomer born in 1962 was only seven at that time. In 1981, when the latter Baby Boomer was 19, Ronald Reagan was riding a wave of patriotism, and punk rocker Sid Vicious was a far cry from folk rocker Joni Mitchell. These disparate formative experiences give lie to psychic unity among Baby Boomers. To gain an understanding of a variety of consumer segments, marketers must devote a few groups to each one of them. A single focus group session is not representative of anything other than a single focus group session.

Cities on the bill

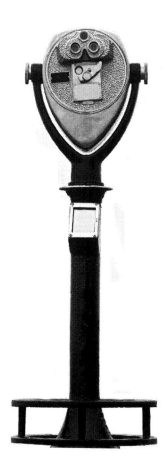

MANY marketing and marketing research directors believe that it is wise to field focus groups in more than one geographical location to be sure they are not missing a range of regional attitudes. There are times when this approach is essential—when a category consists of geographically dispersed buyers with dissimilar psychographic characteristics or when consumers use a brand differently in far-apart locations. Travel to more than two cites in one country is usually a waste of time and money. Focus group moderator Janet Barnhart offers several reasons in a trade article. Among her most convincing arguments are first, focus groups are not meant to be representative samples, so why act as if they are? Second, Americans are a people in motion. A respondent in Pittsburgh today might have been a respondent in Los Angeles last month and could be a respondent in New York next year. Travel only when travel is necessary. For a wide swath of geographical responses, conduct a nationally representative quantitative study. For international research, the same reasoning applies.

6

Watch people do what they do

WE LEARNED in kindergarten that there is a big difference between showing and telling. Respondents in focus groups report on what they do, but is it *actually* what they do? When ice cream consumers say they eat a bowl of ice cream, what size bowl do they choose, and how much is in the bowl? Offer them a few different size bowls, note which one they select, and see how much ice cream they scoop. Be sure to tell these respondents to take their normal portion, not their "in front of strangers" portion. Tell them that twice! As consumers spoon their favorite flavors into their mouths, listen and watch as they characterize the cascade of tastes and textures they experience. Witness toothpaste consumers brush their teeth, ask them what they wish for in flavors and benefits, and notice the areas they miss; these observations can inspire new products. For brands that need to improve their online communications, pay close attention as respondents navigate the brand's web site and narrate the excursion.

As Yogi Berra said, "You can observe a lot by watching."

7

Have consumers interact with people in their lives

AN EXCELLENT way to understand how and why consumers make purchase decisions is to watch them interact with the people who influence these decisions. During interactional research you can observe children ask their parents for their favorite brands and how their parents respond. You can see and hear the ways couples negotiate the purchase of big ticket items like cars, or the decision-making process used by groups of friends as they discuss where to go out for dinner, or how women shop for shoes with their best friend.

In doctor-patient interactional research, the miscues, misreads, and missed opportunities that confound communication and impede better healthcare can be seen and heard. We conducted interactional research among doctors and patients when a client was marketing an innovative prescription contraceptive, but physicians and their patients were stuck in their usual methods. We discovered that physicians assumed their patients were happier with their current contraceptive than they were in reality, so they did not encourage change or offer information about new methods unless asked. Only when the patients in the research mentioned a reservation about their method to the doctor or asked, "What's new in contraception?" did the doctor discuss the new option. Based on this study, the client developed direct-to-consumer communications that sparked patients to inquire of their doctors about new contraception solutions as well as doctor-targeted communications to convince doctors that patients would react positively to the new method they were marketing.

Where you focus makes a difference

A FOCUS group room is not always the ideal environment for reliable information or forthright expression. Consider the degree to which the setting influences the response. Consumers pay more attention to advertising played in a focus group facility than to ads shown on their television at home. The focus room setting can misrepresent how well they understand a message, how strongly they will object to a less-than-logical plot, or how likely they are to accept an approach that is cutting-edge. Respondents are often more relaxed and expressive in natural settings, such as their homes, than in a focus group room. Homes also provide stimuli, such as a medicine cabinet, that reveal otherwise hidden consumer behavior and attitudes.

Many marketing researchers conduct ethnography, which entails observation and interviewing of people in natural settings. Ethnography can be fielded in the form of shop-alongs, where a researcher accompanies a consumer while she shops in her usual store, or as home interviews during which respondents wash their dishes with both your and your competition's brands. If the proj-

Refocusing Focus Groups

ect is in the automotive category, it's worth going for a drive with consumers to watch them use the instrumentation and react to the car in motion. Heinz conducted focus groups on its ketchup in restaurants to learn how people used the brand, including what foods they put it on and how they applied it.

Ethnography often produces findings that could not have been garnered in a focus group room. During ethnographic research on an industrial lubricant, we visited a printer's shop and watched a technician choose the brand that was close within reach. When questioned about why he selected this brand when he had other lubricants in his shop, the technician said that he did not want to take time to walk across the room for another brand (ours), even though it was, in his view, superior. We realized that the power of our brand was more about what was in his mind than what was in the can. We knew we needed to do more to make our brand worth taking a few extra steps.

Observations in focus group facilities can only go so far, so it is sometimes best to go where the respondents are.

Choose the right moderator

SELECTING the person who will moderate the focus groups is one of the most critical decisions that will be made in the planning phase. For some projects, but not all, category experience is an asset. The ability to make respondents feel comfortable, flexibility, attention to detail, listening skills, marketing acumen, writing ability, and chemistry with the research team must be considered. Some marketers prefer moderators whose personal characteristics or experience match the respondents'—a mother interviewing mothers—but this requirement is not always necessary.

James A. Holstein and Jaber F. Gubrium note in their book, *The Active Interview,* that interviewing is a social process and the meaning of the interview is co-created by the interviewer and the respondents. The individual fielding the questions and interacting with respondents is as much a participant in the research as the consumers who have been recruited. That is why choosing the right moderator is so crucial.

Some moderators work independently; others are part of a larger company. In the latter case, invite a Principal of the marketing research company to observe the groups and contribute to the back room analysis and discussion.

10

The Holy Trinity:
Strategy, Tactics, Execution

IN THE marketing industry, "strategy" is the plan, "tactics" are the means by which the plan is delivered, and "execution" is the content of what is delivered—a specific advertisement is an execution. Execution also means the process of getting the strategy and tactic developed, but that won't trouble us here.

Consider the marketing strategy for a new video game. The strategy will specify which consumers the game will target as well as what features, attributes, and benefits they will find appealing. Focus groups are a good place to begin to learn about these things, and only target consumers should be recruited for the sessions. The strategy will include desired respondents' gender, age, and other demographic and psychographic factors, and whether and how often they use certain types of video games that are similar to the new one being marketed. How the game's features, attributes, and benefits will be conveyed to consumers should be reflected in the research. If the advertising for the new video game will be mainly via online or television ads, then the concepts shown should include visuals and graphics that would work in these media; if radio is the main tactical choice, only audio should be exposed. This leads to the content of the advertising, the executions. Words and graphics shown to consumers should represent a wide range of ideas so that a variety of reactions can be obtained. Respondents should be asked for their purchase interest, but questioning should center on comprehension, likes and dislikes, believability of claims, the price/value relationship, and uniqueness versus competition.

11 Be creative

MY COLLEAGUE, Cynthia Weinman, tells this story: Decades ago, a marketing research company dealt creatively with the challenge of assessing NBC's representation of its color broadcast technology when most people owned black and white televisions. It was important to get this right, because more and more people were buying color TVs and NBC needed to demonstrate that it was on the cutting edge of this technology. Several images were in contention: a rainbow, a paintbrush with droplets of colored paints on its bristles, chimes in brilliant hues, a sunset, and a peacock. Since most TV viewers at the time watched black and white televisions, the research company reasoned that the central question was which image best communicated color when seen in black and white. Its creative solution was to conduct the study two ways, with one segment of consumers seeing the graphics in black and white, and another group viewing them in color. The NBC Peacock won because it conveyed color best when seen in black and white. Research design, whether in qualitative or quantitative studies, should fit the learning objective. Creative thinking can make all the difference.

12 Spanning the globe

FOR MANUFACTURERS planning qualitative research cross-culturally, there are special issues beyond the obvious language differences. As Theresa Schreiber and Daryl Gilbert point out in a trade article on international research, you must pay attention to several factors: time zones, holidays, the quality and availability of focus group facilities, technical support, demographic variations, cultural habits and practices, local moderator selection, and translation. The overarching steps to be taken include selecting proven local partners and allocating sufficient time for research planning, design, and execution. An excellent resource for global research, qualitative and quantitative, is *International Marketing Research* by Samuel C. Craig and Susan P. Douglas.

13 | Online focus groups

ONLINE focus groups are increasingly popular among marketers and for good reason: they save time and money, they enable researchers to obtain a national sample of respondents, and they capture consumers who like using their computers to "talk" about their brand experiences. Online applications make it possible to build panels of large numbers of respondents and poll them quickly. Chat rooms, bulletin boards, and blogs have value in monitoring consumer attitudes and behavior. Online focus groups are not, however, a substitute for in-person research. What is expressed is unseen; what is typed is unheard. Respondents' faces, body language, and the inflection of the words they use convey meaning. A smile, a shrug, and a tone of voice are not evident online. Real-time, on-site interaction of the back room observers adds a component to the focus group experience that is not matched online.

Online research has many virtues, and it is an essential tool for 21st century marketing research. However, when it comes to seeing and hearing consumers, as Woody Allen once said, 80 percent of success is showing up.

Part 2

Guide the Guide

Questions of a thousand dreams

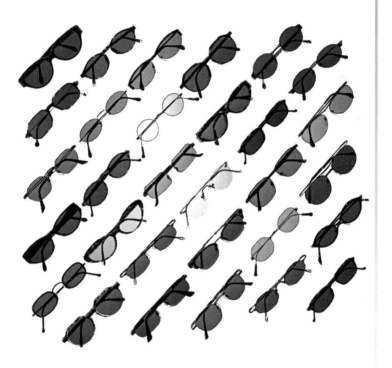

QUALITATIVE research is free flowing compared with other research techniques. When surveys are designed, time limitations and concerns about respondent fatigue constrict the length of the questionnaires. In focus groups, marketers sometimes feel that they can add question after question to a moderator's guide. For example, when the primary research objective is to elicit responses to packaging, manufacturers dream up questions about consumer usage, brand loyalty, advertising, and new products. These requests are understandable; why not take advantage of having captive consumers in a focus group room?

An ideal moderator's guide for a 90-minute session is four to five pages. Yet, I have been pressed to craft guides twice that length in order to answer a multitude of queries. My response is to tell marketers that we will have ample time for the questions but little time for the answers. As a result of some negotiation, the guide is limited to just seven pages! The lesson is learned during the sessions when respondents' answers have to be cut short because the moderator must move rapidly from question to question.

The next time focus groups are planned, clients understand that only some of their dreams can be realized.

Make the warm-up warmer

A FOCUS group always seems to become more productive over the course of the session. The participants become increasingly at ease and they open up more readily as the moderator's questions unfold. Their answers expand and the conversation within the entire group flows more freely. Why not advance this process and allow moderators enough time up front—more than the usual five minutes—to build rapport with the group? One way for the moderator to gain affinity with respondents is to tell them something about herself, such as what she likes most about her job, and then ask the respondents to talk about what they like most about their jobs or their home life. Respondents will relax and reveal more about how and what they think for the duration of the session.

16 The value of being naïve

ANTHROPOLOGISTS are experts at assuming a naïve stance because their job is to take nothing as a given when they observe and interpret exotic, or even well known, cultures. They make the familiar unfamiliar by deconstructing everyday behaviors, and their fundamental questions can be revelatory when applied to consumer beliefs, attitudes, and behavior. In their book, *Doing Anthropology in Consumer Research,* anthropologists Patricia Sunderland and Rita Denny pose the question, "What is coffee?" They note that by stepping back and making this query naïvely, it is revealed that coffee is a beverage with multiple connotations about fashion, relaxation, strength, tradition, and much more.

During qualitative research on a breakfast cereal, we asked respondents what breakfast *is*. We learned that breakfast is an in-between, ritual-like time when certain personal transformations occur. Early morning is a transitional period; consumers move over a threshold from sleep to waking, from their private to public self. The specific breakfast cereal brand they consume during the transition is an essential component of their transformational experience. In this research, we discovered that our brand's sensate attributes of sweetness and crunch made respondents feel happy, optimistic, and even joyful, promising a positive beginning to their day. This is the stuff of effective advertising.

17

To get respondents to talk, get them to draw

IMAGES in the form of photographs, drawings, or other formats enable respondents to express ideas and emotions that may not surface easily or naturally even with well-crafted questions. The use of what psychologists call projective techniques is a powerful springboard for focus group discussions.

One projective method, called the ZMET (Zaltman Metaphor Elicitation Technique) named for its inventor, Gerald Zaltman, uses visual stimuli to tap customer attitudes and feelings. In the ZMET and similar approaches, respondents select from a pile of images during a focus group or are given pre-session homework assignments to create collages that they bring to the interviews. The graphics help moderators access consumer thinking in ways that direct questions cannot. The process can inspire advertising ideas when respondents *show* how dandruff feels—a snowstorm—or illustrate a new stem-like product delivery system with an elephant's trunk.

A related procedure is what my company calls the Color Crayon Technique. Before exposure to packaging and other questioning, respondents use crayons to draw package faces of a brand and its competitors from memory. As they sketch the colors and shapes, brand equities materialize. Manufacturers considering changes may learn that they need to retain certain graphics on their packaging and be aware of design elements that resonate among consumers on their competitors' packaging.

Don't take "no" for an answer

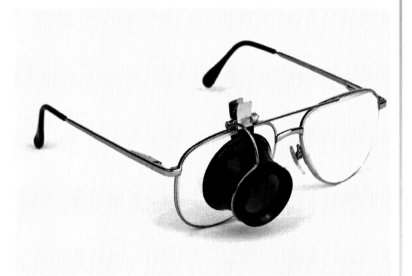

WHEN consumers are asked about their level of purchase interest in a product, and they respond, "Probably not," the reasons behind their position are usually highly informative. Many respondents say that the product is too expensive. They mean that, to them, it's not worth the cost. By asking consumers what the product would need to be or do to be worth the price, marketers can learn about improvements that could increase the value of the product and justify the price proposed.

Don't take "yes" for an answer

CONSUMERS in focus groups often say, "I would probably buy it," when asked if they would purchase an item based on a new product concept.

Would they really?

The next question should be, "What would the product described in the concept replace?" Respondents' "Probably Would Buy" sometimes drops to a "Might or Might Not Buy" if they must give up or use less of the brand they currently use. Consumers who use a certain shampoo daily may not want to change that habit when they think twice about it. The query, "Is this new product *better* than the one you currently use?" can prompt respondents to rethink their declared purchase intent or make statements that kindle selling ideas for the new product.

20 Think like a dentist: Probe deeply but gently

IT HURTS when the dentist probes, but this procedure is the only way a cavity can be remedied. So it is with consumer interviews. Sensitive topics are best addressed with special care.

In a study on an over-the-counter day-after-sex emergency contraceptive, we interviewed women in a focus room setting individually. Our moderator asked them to tell stories about the times they had unprotected sexual intercourse. To help mitigate the sensitivity of this very personal experience, the moderator told them to imagine what music might be playing and what the sky looked like the morning after. These questions enabled the moderator to probe gently and without pain. The women's vivid and stirring descriptions led to evocative brand advertising.

21 Think like a detective: Get the truth

WE'VE ALL seen television dramas in which a hard-as-nails police detective interrogates a suspect relentlessly until he finally breaks and confesses to the crime. I don't advocate threats of bodily harm, but a moderator should press for the truth when respondents make suspicious statements or are evasive during questioning. Respondents should be pushed to provide real-life support for their claimed behavior: "You said you change your air freshener once a month. When, exactly, do you change it? How do you keep track?" Even a simple, but incredulous "Really?" from the moderator can spur consumers towards revelations.

When leading is a bad thing

"WHEN did you stop beating your wife?" This is obviously a leading question that carries an underlying assumption. Attorneys with a pre-determined agenda find these modes of inquiry useful, but moderators must avoid them. Leading questions in qualitative research direct respondents down a path to particular answers and undermine the quest for objective learning and insight. Most professional moderators are savvy enough to steer clear of questions like, "What are your major concerns about this advertising?" and ask instead, "What did you like most and least about this advertising?" Back room observers need to be attentive to moderator missteps and send in a note to the moderator to be sure he or she is aware that too much direction was given in a question.

23 When "grayish-yellow-green" equals green

THE WAY we use words to categorize the world in which we live reveals our cognitive processes. It also demonstrates the strategies we adopt to deal with problems we encounter. Understanding how people classify certain experiences has marketing value. For example, asking focus group respondents to describe types of headaches sparks new ways of selling a brand. How else could "tension headache" have been invented?

The 1948 movie, *Mr. Blandings Builds His Dream House*, illustrates how differently people categorize colors. In one scene, Mrs. Blandings (played by Myrna Loy) discusses the paint colors that she has in mind with a painting contractor and his underling. Mrs. Blandings goes into minute detail as she walks the contractor through each room.

Mrs. Blandings: *Now, first, the living room. I want it to be a soft green.*

Contractor: *Uh huh.*

Mrs. Blandings: *Not as blue-green as a robin's egg.*

Contractor: *No.*

Mrs. Blandings: *But not as yellow-green as daffodil buds.*

Contractor: *Uh huh.*

Mrs. Blandings: *Now, the only sample I could get is a little too yellow. But don't let whoever does it go to the other extreme and get it too blue.*

Contractor: *No.*

Mrs. Blandings: *It should be a sort of grayish-yellow-green.*

Contractor: *Uh huh.*

After Mrs. Blandings completes the walk-through, with the same level of detailed description for each room, she leaves the contractor and his underling to handle another issue. The contractor turns to his underling:

Contractor: *You got that, Charlie?*

Charlie: *Red, green, blue, yellow, white.*

Contractor: *Check.*

By uncovering color perceptions and terminology, paint manufacturers can create and name colors that match consumers' imaginative thinking.

24

Climb the emotional ladder

FOCUS group respondents do not arrive at a session ready and willing to lay their innermost thoughts on the conference table. They need help. Often the best place to begin is with a concrete experience followed by probing questions that give respondents a boost up the emotional ladder. Example:

Question: *How do you feel when you have a cold?*

Answer: *Achy.*

Question: *How does feeling achy make you feel?*

Answer: *Weak and helpless.*

Question: *How do you wish you could feel when you feel weak and helpless?*

Answer: *Strong and powerful!*

Enter the brand with the strength to give consumers the power they need to get back to their lives.

Take a walk on Sesame Street

THERE is a song on the long-running children's television program, *Sesame Street,* that goes like this:

One of these things is not like the others;
One of these things just doesn't belong.
Can you tell which thing is not like the others
By the time I finish my song?

This song refers to a simple classification technique, using three objects, known in psychology as triadic sorting. It is an excellent means of accessing how consumers think about competitive brands. Respondents are first instructed to group together two out of three related brands based on an attribute they share, and then to discuss their similarities and contrast them with the third brand. The pairings of brands in opposition to a third are rotated until all permutations are covered. Consumers may link brands based upon package design in the first grouping, on efficacy in the second grouping, and on delivery systems in the third grouping.

Consider three fast food chains for an example of triadic sorting. Do consumers see McDonald's and Burger King as innovators, and view Wendy's as traditional? Do Burger King and Wendy's suggest fresh and McDonald's frozen?

The best way to use this data depends on which competitor is most threatening to your brand or is a vulnerable source for market share.

26
Talk to people in love (and out of love) with a brand

CONSUMERS often progress through a romance-like series of phases with brands: discovery, anticipation, passion, fulfillment, routine, disappointment, and change. Speaking with consumers in each of the stages of their brand relationship can help build and protect a brand's market share. The passion that respondents proclaim when they are in love with a brand can be used to motivate less enthusiastic buyers. Understanding why respondents fell out of love with a brand can safeguard the brand from future rejection by current consumers.

The management of a Philadelphia radio station wanted to encourage light listeners to increase their listening time. We recruited people from the target segment as well as heavy listeners who had increased their commitment to the station recently. Interviews with heavy users suggested that reminding people of how the station positively impacts their mood could encourage light users to increase the time spent tuned in to the station.

27 Deprive respondents

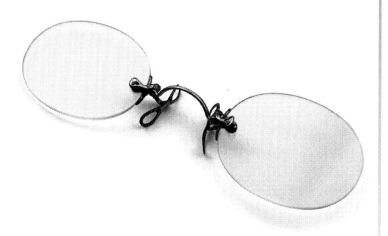

DEPRIVING respondents of the opportunity to buy products in an entire category leads to knowledge about substitutions. Tell mustard consumers to imagine that mustard is no longer on the market. Do they opt for ketchup or taco sauce? Maybe you have a new line extension. Deprivation can also be examined by telling respondents not to use their regular brand for two weeks before a focus group, to keep a diary, and then report on their experience when they participate in the interview session. This exercise is one that consumers are surprisingly willing to do. Their stories can lead to new products and advertising ideas.

You can obtain a sense of your brand's strength against competition by asking respondents what they would do if their brand were not available in their preferred size or usual store. Would they select another size or buy another brand? If respondents would travel to another store to purchase your brand, you have a loyal customer. If they would choose another brand, be sure you have consumers' most desired sizes in stock—and work harder to differentiate your brand.

28 Travel back in time to see the future

GUIDING consumers through their past can yield future ideas. A manufacturer was exploring new product possibilities for its carpet freshener. Respondents were asked to reflect back on their lives and tell stories about their experiences with things or places that seem "fresh." Here is some of what they said:

- Raking leaves at my grandparents' house on an autumn day, the air clean and pure. I felt so alive. It was exhilarating.

- The smell of flowers at my communion. My grandmother gave us all flowers—carnations and daisies. I was overwhelmed by the fragrance of the flowers. I felt happy, proud, excited.

- My mom's cooking: homemade pizza, making tomatoes into sauce. I felt content, relaxed.

- Sleeping on sheets my mom dried on the line. A smell, but not a smell . . . just clean.

Respondents were then asked to invent new products for the brand. Among their many suggestions (paraphrased to protect confidentiality):

- Fresh Lift, a "rake" that lifts embedded dirt before vacuuming

- Old Carpet Freshener, which restores body and color vibrancy to aging carpets

- Fresh and Soft, which makes carpets smell great and feel softer

Not all of these products flowed directly from the life histories, but by taking respondents back to the sensation of fresh, we inspired them to create fresh ideas.

29 Travel to different dimensions

CONSUMERS experience brands in psychological, social, and functional dimensions.

We conducted qualitative research on a brand in the sore throat medicine category, and we wanted to take a deep dive into the trust consumers felt in our brand. This study consisted of in-depth interviews with individual consumers in a focus room facility. Before arriving at the session, respondents were instructed to create collages with images that depicted what a sore throat feels like as well as other collages that illustrated their emotions when a sore throat is relieved. During the sessions, respondents were asked to reflect upon distinctive experiences with pain and relief and to tell stories about positive and negative trust episodes in their lives. They were also asked to talk about the social implications of sickness, and to discuss the functional properties of the sore throat brands they preferred.

This research helped us discover several dimensions of trust: trust based on individual needs, like "I trust that I will feel myself again" and deep feelings about caregivers; trust based on social interaction needs, like "I trust that I will be able to get out and be in the world again"; trust based on proven experience with the brand and its ability to soothe a sore throat.

Advertising based on the findings of this research broke persuasion test records for the brand.

Plant seeds

ONE technique to ensure that respondents arrive at focus groups on new products with plenty to say is to send them a product sample two weeks before the session. Instruct them to use it, keep a diary, and take digital photographs of themselves and, if appropriate, their family members or friends using the product. These "seeding studies" animate focus groups. The sessions are richer in content than those in which consumers read concepts and imagine how a product would feel in their hands, work on their laundry, or taste in their mouths—and fit into their lives.

31 Pull triggers

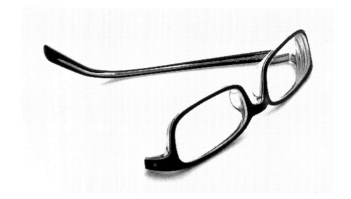

CONSUMERS often explore new categories and try new brands as a consequence of changes in their lives. "Trigger events" like a fiftieth birthday or an illness may stimulate first-time consideration of certain types of wellness products. Children heading off to college might lead parents to consider remodeling unused rooms. Group discussions with consumers about their lifecycle passages—and their purchase decisions during these times—are illuminating.

How many concepts can we show?

ONE of the most frequently asked questions when planning focus groups is: "How many concepts can we show to the respondents?" My answer: as few as possible and no more than five.

Whether exposing new product ideas, advertising, or packaging designs, keep in mind that the stimuli pile up on one another and the content becomes cumulative. When respondents don't get the message in the first commercial but "play it back" as if they heard it for the first time in the second, it means that the second time they were exposed to the message it registered. Rotating the order of the concepts helps diminish this problem, but the cumulative impact applies; over the course of a day of focus groups, you're securing "clean" learning only on the first concept. What is worse is that after exposure to a large number of concepts, respondents' minds become muddled and their reactions aren't worth hearing. Extending the length of the focus groups to accommodate more concepts is not a solution. Whether a group is 90 minutes or two hours long, muddle is muddle.

Part 3
Listening and Observing

The Rashomon perspective

THE 1950 Japanese film, *Rashomon,* recounts a woman's rape and the murder of her husband as seen through the eyes and conflicting interpretations of four different witnesses, including those of the deceased husband. The film deals with alternate versions of the truth as expressed by people with particular self-interests. Observers in the back room see focus groups in a way that is similar to the witnesses in *Rashomon.* Self-interest, whether conscious or unconscious, also has an impact on their interpretations. In *Rashomon,* each of the witnesses had something to hide, protect, or champion—honor, shame, theft, skill. Focus group observers are influenced by personal bias, brand history, and management edicts. While they may seek the truth, it is a truth that is nevertheless shaped by these factors. Focus group observers should realize that the image in the mirror is often their own reflection; as they look at the glass, they should try to see past themselves. Complete objectivity is seldom possible in marketing research, but acknowledging bias will enable manufacturers and advertising agency executives to separate their interpretation of the truth from the other versions of the truth expressed by consumers.

34

When their lips say "yes" and their eyes say "no"

IN HIS book, *Blink,* Malcolm Gladwell writes about behavioral scientists who "read minds" by studying facial expressions, even "microexpressions" that occur in a small fraction of a second. These movements are involuntary; they are not controlled by the person emitting them, yet they reveal otherwise unstated emotions and attitudes. Behavioral scientists have systematic ways of observing and recording these expressions, and special expertise is required to catch them—and interpret them accurately. Focus group observers, even though they lack special training, should pay close attention to respondents' facial and body movements because they provide clues as to whether consumers are saying what they really think and feel.

35 Just watch

FOR OBSERVERS who are not experts in deciphering respondents' facial and body language, one way to gain a sense of these microexpressions is to shut off the sound in the back room for a few minutes. Watch the respondents closely. The silence will heighten your awareness of their non-verbal behavior. You may notice that while a television commercial is being shown, respondents smile, nod, or look away. These movements divulge reactions that consumers may choose not to verbalize or that are unconscious, and they present a reason for the moderator to challenge a verbal response. By shutting off the sound for a short time, you'll be more sensitive to these kinds of signals as the focus groups progress.

Just listen

DEBORAH Tannen is a sociolinguist who believes that the meaning we convey in spoken language is not only in the words but also in their context and delivery. In Tannen's book, *You're Wearing That?* she points out that when a mother says to her daughter, "You're not going to wear *that*, are you?" she is not asking a question but rather making a critical comment. In focus groups, as in life, both words and inflection are complex components of communication. Listening carefully, occasionally with eyes closed, will make you more attuned to multiple levels of meaning.

The difference between clean and fresh

DURING a focus group on toilet bowl cleaners, my colleagues and I were stupefied as one respondent after another left one of the primary benefits of their regular brand off their list of most important brand attributes. The benefit—"leaves the bathroom fresh"—was a centerpiece of advertising, supported by millions of dollars, for every toilet bowl cleaner brand these consumers bought. Respondents talked about how clean their toilets were; why didn't they mention the benefit that we marketers, and our competition, felt was so important?

Those of us in the back room were being too literal about the meaning of the words we heard. We interpreted them at face value. We needed to explore the possibility that "clean" not only meant free of dirt, but also meant fresh smelling. The benefit of "leaves the bathroom fresh" may have been expressed indirectly by respondents with a single word—"clean"—that held several meanings for them but only one for the marketing professionals.

This kind of analysis, with attention to connotation and context, can be applied to many words uttered in focus groups. When we take a word solely at its literal meaning, we can miss critical information. Words like "clean" and "fresh" are rich in connotation. By attending to the layered meanings of these kinds of words, we comprehend what our respondents are really saying.

38 The dog didn't bark

OBSERVERS should notice what is *not* being said as well as what is being said by respondents. In the story, *Silver Blaze*, Sherlock Holmes observed that a dog did not bark during the commission of a crime, which meant that the perpetrator of the crime was familiar to the dog. If focus group respondents do not bring up a feature that you think is important, perhaps it is not important to them. If they do not mention advertising graphics that the ad agency creative team thinks have impact, maybe the impact is only in the minds of the creative team.

When will this product be on the market?

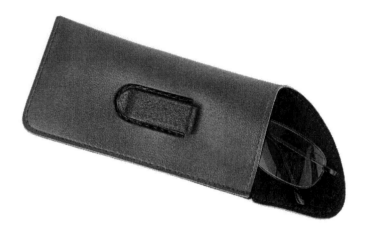

THE FOCUS group ends and the moderator says, "thank you" to the respondents. At that moment, observers sometimes are fortuitously treated to a clue as to how appealing a product innovation is to consumers. Take note if participants linger in the interview room to discuss the topic further with the moderator. Does anyone ask, "Are they really coming out with that product?" This informal conversation may suggest that interest in the offerings consumers discussed for the past 90 minutes is greater than was expressed during the session.

Listen and observe consistently

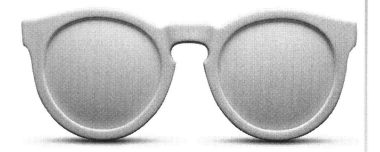

SITTING behind a focus room mirror, listening and watching consumers answer questions hour after hour can lead to an attention deficit. An observer is riveted to the proceedings inside the focus group interview room. Then an email pops up on her laptop, she reads the email, and responds. In the moments that her attention was drawn away from the focus group session, she may have missed a choice consumer phrase that would be valuable for advertising. Or, a statement from a respondent might have been made that contradicts what he said earlier in the session. Selective listening yields selected findings. Time taken away from the office to attend focus groups should be time devoted to the sessions. Emails, phone calls, and other business should be handled during breaks.

Part 4

Back Room Conduct

Why are so many focus group respondents fat?

SOME marketing professionals have an overly narrow view of who their typical customer is or, even worse, judge focus group respondents based on their physical appearance or manner of speaking. This attitude is not only myopic; it is also detrimental to business development. Consumers in a brand's target are worth listening to, even if they look, think, and act differently than you might wish or expect. It is tempting for observers to sit behind the focus room mirror and comment derisively about a respondent's weight, clothing, or hairstyle. These remarks induce laughter among colleagues and engender back room collegiality. But, beyond being cruel, such comments are counter-productive. Personal remarks about respondents are distracting, and they can be sexist, ageist, or racist. Such statements might cause observers to dismiss the reactions of people they judge harshly or give undue credence to respondents they see as attractive. Back room comments about respondents' physical appearance or demeanor rather than about what they say lead to prejudices—negative or positive—that do not belong behind the mirror.

42 Talk while you listen

CHATTER in the back room sometimes drowns out the voices of the respondents in the focus group room. For most of the session, full attention should be given to the action on the other side of the mirror. However, on occasion, what is being discussed in the back room may be more valuable than what is being said in the interview session. A respondent's statement may spark a conversation among the observer team that leads to a new concept, which can, in turn, be exposed in the next focus group that day. Back room talk is, in this sense, part of the overall research. The key is to keep these discussions short and postpone longer conversations until the break.

There is a viewing option for team members who prefer to filter out comments from their colleagues: watch the sessions from a remote location using an online service like FocusVision.

Messy houses are interesting houses

FOCUS group sessions, like houses, are more interesting when they are a little messy.

The moderator's guide is informed by client needs and wants; it is crafted by the marketing research company, and revised several times by the entire team before the day of the research. Marketers sometimes regard the guide the same way that fundamentalists read the Bible—literally. The guide is best viewed as a compendium of the questions that need to be answered, rather than as a script. In fact, deviating from the guide can yield treasure, especially when respondents say something completely unexpected. Advertising anthropologist Timothy de Waal Malefyt argues that "confusion and surprise" often generate the most profound insights in qualitative research.

One of the virtues of focus groups is flexibility. If a question is not eliciting the desired range or depth of responses, change it. Add new questions. Follow unanticipated leads.

The folly of tallies

MORE times than I can count, I have witnessed brand managers totaling up the "Definitely Would Buy" responses and the "Probably Would Buy" responses from consumers who have been asked about their purchase intent after reading a new product concept or viewing a television advertising storyboard. One of the cardinal rules of focus groups is: *Numbers don't count.* The sample is too small, the setting is artificial, and people don't always mean what they say when a moderator asks them about purchase intent. It is a major risk to take to the bank, let alone to senior corporate management, the number of focus group respondents who say they intend to purchase a product.

Well-fed observers are happy observers

Refocusing Focus Groups

A DAY of focus group research is long and the observers in the back room must be fed. Meals are either pre-selected by the research firm or they are ordered by the observers from menu booklets representing local restaurants. The food requirements of observers must be met: vegetarian, vegan, gluten-free, kosher—whatever is desired. In cases where food is not pre-ordered, the team must agree on a single restaurant source for the sake of convenience and timely delivery. Negotiations as to the choice of restaurant are often lengthy; a marketing manager, advertising agency account executive, or research manager must seize leadership lest the order not be filled soon enough, resulting in a late arriving meal. The back room crowd can get ugly.

To stave off the boredom that inevitably results from watching even the most scintillating respondents talk over the course of eight hours, focus group facilities provide snacks. Small bowls of M&M's, nuts, pretzels, and wrapped candies are placed around the observation room. Some facilities offer fresh baked chocolate chip cookies. In the afternoon or evening, a plate of fruit with cheese and crackers may be set on a counter near the observers.

It is virtually impossible for members of the team to be hungry while watching a focus group. But, if the food is not to their liking, their mood may darken and so will their perception of the quality of the moderating, the honesty of the respondents, and the depth of insight offered by their colleagues. The person managing the research project must keep in mind that well-fed observers are happy and productive observers.

46 Herding cats

A CHIEF operating officer from a manufacturing company who had recently emigrated to the advertising business used the term, "herding cats," to describe the challenge of managing creative individuals with conflicting agendas. Marketing researchers face a similar challenge when dealing with their clients. Corporate research managers have internal clients—marketing executives. Supplier research professionals serve corporate research managers, brand managers, and advertising agency executives. It's a tough job, not dissimilar from shepherding a herd of cats. Treats help. In marketing research, treats are represented by excellent listening skills, honest communication of what can and cannot be accomplished, regular progress reports, and sensitivity to the pressures clients face. These practices do not guarantee that all of the constituencies will move in the same direction at the same time, but they will help get the team's attention.

Part 5

Interpretation

The Henny Youngman question

HENNY Youngman was a mid-20th century comedian with a decidedly mid-20th century sense of humor. One of his better known one-liners was, "Somebody asked me how my wife was. I said, 'Compared to what?'" Mr. Youngman's rejoinder is a reminder that questions like, "How likely are you to purchase this product based on the commercial you just saw?" omit a major component of consumer behavior: comparison shopping. To fully explore the decision-making thought process after respondents view an advertisement, show them a shelf-set with an array of competitive brands. Now, with competitors in sight, ask consumers about their buying decision and elicit the thinking behind their purchase-intent declaration.

48 When consumers lie to themselves

JONNY Lang is an American blues-rock songwriter and guitarist. Among the lyrics in the title song of his 1997 album, *Lie to Me,* are: *"Lie to me and tell me everything is all right. . . . I'll just try to make believe that everything, everything you're telling me is true . . ."*

Human beings sometimes prefer to live a lie rather than deal with an uncomfortable truth. As marketing researchers, we must recognize when this happens in focus groups and understand how it impacts our findings.

Four 40-something women entered an interview room for a focus group. During the session, they spoke about taking long walks, other exercise regimens, and their efforts to eat right. Not one woman mentioned a weight problem, yet all of these consumers were significantly overweight. Per the recruit, the respondents were loyal users of a breakfast cereal with a name that connotes nutritional goodness but contains ingredients that give it a sweet taste and substantial calories. The consumers described the brand as "good for them"; they loved its taste, but, even more, they praised its health benefits. These women did not read the brand's nutrition label. If they had, they would have known that the cereal is light in nutrition and heavy in sugar. They allowed themselves to be deluded by the healthy sounding brand name. These consumers wanted to live the lie that the brand was good for them *because* they loved the taste. The brand name gave them permission to lie to themselves by implying that eating it was consistent with the way they managed their health. These women didn't know it, but they had a lot in common with Jonny Lang.

Stop making sense

MARKETING books, articles, and presentations expound on the necessity for advertising to appeal to both the hearts and minds of consumers. Although plenty of advertising tugs at the heart with no reference to concrete promises (consider perfume ads), and some ads lack emotion entirely ("reduces itching by 99%" comes to mind), most advertising contains a mix of substance and sentiment. Single men who wish to look younger and more attractive conceal their grey hair with the brand that promises just the right amount of color; automotive ads speak to myriad consumer needs for performance, elegance, environmental responsibility, and social status; mothers buy brands based upon assurances that their children will be happy consuming a great tasting fruit drink that has the advantage of vitamin-fortification.

It is anomalous that rational and emotional messages, so often intertwined in advertisements, are sometimes separated in research. An advertising agency executive sent the following email message as we prepared for research on brand positioning: "We would like to make the accompanying visuals without emotion. This will eliminate any variables that might influence the reading that we get. If we include pictures that have an emotional connotation, they might sway people's reactions and therefore influence the responses that we get on the concepts themselves."

My response to the ad agency's suggestion was this: Advertising for the brand in question will not be purely rational. If we show a purely rational concept, consumer emotions will be left out of the conversation. Since we know from neurological studies that rational and emotional reactions often drive one another, separating them in marketing research will not address the impact of their combined strength. Research findings based exclusively on rational concepts will not just be wrong, they will misdirect advertising development.

Concepts for advertising research should include words and images that convey both the rational and emotional sides of the brand equation. The terms for these kinds of concepts vary— "adcepts" and "ad-like-objects" are among the most widely used descriptions. This integrated approach will engage consumers' hearts and minds.

50

Rationalization is the most common cause of heart attacks

MANY of us say, "I'm doing all I can to get into shape, but I'm too busy at work and with my family to walk 30 minutes a day and eat responsibly. Besides, all the nutritional information out there is complicated, and I don't have time to make salad for dinner every night." And so we live our lives—until we receive a wake up call in the form of acute chest pain.

People in focus groups rationalize too. Ask a person why he doesn't take vitamins every day and he goes on and on about the reasons, many of which make complete sense. That's why the word "rational" is the root of the word "rationalization." Moderators need to press respondents to discover what lies beneath their rationalizations. Are consumers not taking their vitamins daily because they don't believe daily consumption is important to their health? If that is the case, marketers must elevate the reasons for taking vitamins every day in consumers' minds.

51 The art of interpretation

FOCUS groups on mothers' attitudes towards children's cereal brands led to an unexpected insight about the emotional drivers of their shopping experience.

We asked our respondents to reflect back on times, years before, when they had shopped with their own moms for cereals. We learned that many of them had happy memories of shopping trips when they were allowed to participate in brand selection. They recalled how powerful they felt, and how much they appreciated their mom for granting them this privilege. As these mothers talked, they realized that they could have that same experience with their children, especially because they knew they ate sugary cereal as children and turned out just fine. We concluded that our brand could be about the *relationship* between mother and child. Making cereal shopping enjoyable as a shared decision-making process would be a rite of childhood for kids, and moms would feel good about empowering their children. Our interpretation of the focus group sessions led, not to what was inside the cereal box, but what was inside the hearts of mothers.

Brands often have meaning for consumers that is so deeply embedded in their psyches that traditional interviews will not access it. In his book, *The Culture Code*, Clotaire Rapaille describes techniques that enable him to discover the symbols and codes that consumers associate with certain brands and categories. His focus groups, conducted over a three-hour period, combine three methods described earlier in this book—naïve questioning, visual representation, and personal histories. In one case history, Rapaille summarizes his work on the Jeep Wrangler. He found that for Americans, the Jeep vehicle represents the Western plains and is symbolized by a horse. Rapaille convinced Jeep executives to redesign the Wrangler with round headlights instead of square ones to mimic the eyes of a horse—and sales rose.

Penetrating, imaginative interpretation of focus groups often leads to brand-building insights.

52 Marketing is cultural

ANTHROPOLOGIST Grant McCracken believes that ignoring culture, which he defines as "the body of ideas, emotions, and activities that make up the life of the consumer," places corporations at extreme risk. Focus groups are an ideal venue to explore what I call "culturalgraphics," a portrait of the deep, often symbolic meaning of consumer customs, rules for behavior, and beliefs. For example, "Thanksgiving" denotes a holiday on the calendar. Its cultural connotations are vast: an idyllic Norman Rockwell–like gathering of family and friends, a day to appreciate all that we have, permission to overindulge in food, a special occasion for cooks to showcase their abilities, a time to reflect on our national history, long, traffic-clogged trips on the highway, college football games, and so on. Each of these meanings has potential applications for marketing brands during the Thanksgiving holiday.

One of the primary uses of focus groups is the preliminary assessment of advertising. Marketers interested in respondents' purchase intent, and little else, miss opportunities for a complete understanding of how their advertising connects with consumers on psychological and cultural levels. Advertising informs us and is informed by our culture. Ads reflect who we are and, at the same time, present an image of who we want to be. Attention should be paid as to how well respondents identify with an advertisement. Aspirational advertising can over-shoot. Consumers might not have an affinity with a stunning 25-year-old woman cleaning a $200,000 kitchen. Similarly, advertising that celebrates a culture of consumption could be an affront to shoppers who view themselves as financially challenged. Focus groups, with their opportunities for cross conversation among respondents, provide a setting for discovering whether advertising stories are relatable for target customers.

53

Why findings from focus groups may not match those of survey respondents

TWENTY is too small a number for statistical projection. That limitation, plus the very presence of a moderator and fellow consumers in a focus group room, explains why focus group observations may not correlate with the results from a carefully constructed questionnaire administered online to 200 people.

It's that simple.

Why does the second focus group contradict the first one?

THE first session begins. The respondents react positively to virtually every new product concept they see. You're elated. After so much work, consumers are telling you that you have winning ideas. The next session begins. The respondents hate virtually every new product concept they see. You're confused, disheartened, depressed. What is happening? Which session was right? Will the next two sessions agree with the first one or the second one? Or, will all of the sessions yield different findings?

Any given focus group consists of a small number people who fit certain specifications. Even if another group, or another three groups, meet the same specifications, it is possible that the group composition will vary in ways you have not imagined. The screener is designed to capture the "right" people for the sessions and keep the "wrong" people out. It includes questions about age, gender, brand use, and other "hard" attributes, and it may contain inquiries on psychographic characteristics. However, the screener is extremely unlikely to have uncovered the fact that the five respondents in group one are obsessive compulsives and the five respondents in group two suffer from oppositional defiant disorder.

It is possible that one group will include a charismatic person who steers the session and has a particularly positive view of the world and your ideas. In the next group, you might find a highly critical respondent with a negative disposition who brings the group down. Quantitative studies obviate many of these issues because people with idiosyncratic dispositions are represented in proportion to their number in the general population. The luck of the draw, the time of day, and other uncontrollable, exogenous factors can also result in differences among focus groups.

The best approach to managing the ups and downs of focus groups is to listen to the respondents' likes and dislikes and their reasoning, and not be overly focused on variations across sessions.

The customer is not always right

RESPONDENTS occasionally give bad advice. They may tell a peanut butter manufacturer that combining jelly and peanut butter in a jar sounds good and that they would buy the new product. The problem with this notion is that a company that makes the best tasting peanut butter may make awful tasting jelly. Introduction of a combined product could damage the reputation of the peanut butter maker and crush their peanut butter brand sales. Manufacturers must distinguish between the marketing initiatives that focus group respondents recommend and what is good for the brand. Consumers are the source of a manufacturer's business; they are not marketing experts. Manufacturers must listen to consumers' needs and wants, but keep in mind that they, not their customers, are the stewards of the brand.

Smart marketers know bad research results are as valuable as good ones

MY CLIENTS sometimes say, "When we have completed these focus groups we can move ahead to the next stage." I reply, "Not so fast. We may learn that we have more work to do before we move to the next stage." On occasion, all the new product concepts or advertising ideas exposed in focus groups are weak or confusing or off-putting. The research may suggest that it is prudent to pause and take a hard look at the ideas produced to date. New efforts may be needed. The sinking feeling marketers have as they witness consumers trash their ideas and then realize that more work is needed is preferable to the sinking feeling they would have if they introduced sub-par products or advertising.

Part 6

Conclusions and Resolutions

Net impressions and considered reactions

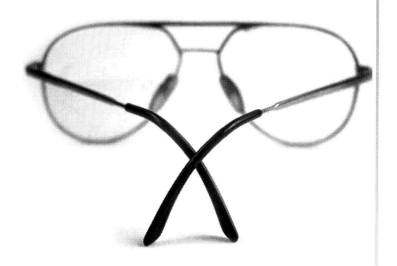

A DAY of focus groups should conclude with a round robin summary of observers' main observations and their tentative conclusions. Begin the discussion with the moderator, who has been the closest listener and is usually the most objective member of the team. Then each team member should offer one finding or insight that he or she has found particularly compelling. After reviewing these impressions, it is best to delay further discussion until at least 24 hours after the last focus group in the series. This provides enough time for the events of the sessions to settle in the observers' minds and for new thinking to emerge. The team members should share their final thoughts before the research company issues its final report.

Never use focus groups as the basis for decision-making

WE'VE established that twenty respondents is not a representative sample, even when they have similar demographic and psychographic profiles. The interaction of the respondents with the moderator and with one another in a focus group room is not akin to real-world reactions to a brand on a store shelf or to advertising on television, on radio, in print, or online. No matter how good or bad the results are in a focus group, remember that the goal of qualitative research is insight, not measurement. The standard caveat in our focus group reports is: "As is the case with all qualitative research, the results should be considered indicative rather than conclusive, due to the small number of respondents."

59

Agree on what comes next.
Sometimes it's more focus groups

FOCUS groups can provide direction for advertising strategies and input for how to frame a new product concept; however, changes to a brand strategy and product innovations must be assessed definitively before moving into the marketplace. Quantitative research is often the best next step after focus groups. When too many questions remain unanswered, further qualitative research should be planned.

The final report: Let it be

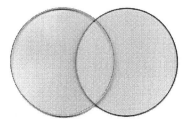

A MARKETING research company is hired to execute a well-designed study and deliver a report on the findings. There are occasions when the research company offers a point-of-view that is different from that of clients who were present at the same sessions. Clients may be tempted to edit the report to reflect their own observations and conclusions. This is antithetical to the use of an independent firm. The focus group report should contain the research company's objective findings and recommendations. The report can be contested or ignored, but it should not be compromised.

Acknowledgements

FOCUS group research is highly collaborative. Most of the examples in this book reflect the hard work and keen insights of my clients and colleagues in marketing, marketing research, and advertising. I acknowledge their contributions to the research described here.

For many excellent suggestions and stimulating conversations that informed the text of this book, I want to express my gratitude to all of my colleagues at Weinman Schnee Morais, especially Cynthia Weinman, and to WSM's kind readers of an early draft of this book: Abbe Fabian, Renee Feldman, Michael Kushner, and Chris Szczepanski. I wish to thank Bob Schnee, Leslie Tucker, Timothy de Waal Malefyt, and Arnold Spector for enlightening discussions on qualitative research, Lisa Lenovitz Eaton for her discerning eye, and Arnold Pedowitz for his contractual expertise. The people at Paramount Market Publishing understood the concept of this book instantly and helped bring it to print: Doris Walsh, Anne Kilgore, and James Madden. Special thanks must be extended to Anne for her inspired choice of graphics and overall imaginative design.

My wife, Jane Morais, has a PhD in French, but knows her way around a sentence in English. Her editorial mind and eye, not to mention her monumental patience, made this book a better read.

Any errors or omissions in this book are my responsibility alone.

SOME of the content of this book was drawn from previously published articles written by the author alone or in collaboration with colleagues. These articles include:

"Refocusing Focus Groups." *Alert!,* January 2010.

"Spanning the Irrational Divide." Published simultaneously in *Adweek, Brandweek,* and *Mediaweek,* June 22, 2009.

"Business Ethnography and the Discipline of Anthropology." *Quirk's Marketing Research Review,* February 2009.

"Interactional Physician-Patient Research: A Path to Better Medical and Marketing Outcomes." *Product Management Today,* December 2007. (with Janet Barnhart).

"X-Groups: Truth or Dare in Focus Groups." *Visions,* April 2004.

"What Are They Really Saying?" *Quirk's Marketing Research Review,* January 2003.

"Getting More Golden Eggs Without Killing the Goose." *Quirk's Marketing Research Review,* December 2003. (with Cara Woodland and Arnold Spector)

"What Boomer Generation?" *Brandweek,* October 7, 2002. (with Debra Goodman)

"The End of Focus Groups." *Quirk's Marketing Research Review,* May 2001.

"Analytical Ideation: Power Brainstorming." *Brandweek,* January 15, 2001.

"Behind the Looking Glass: Making Focus Groups More Effective." *Product Management Today,* March 2000. (with Robert K. Schnee)

"Reaching Asian-Americans Not a One-Dimension Task." *Advertising Age,* February 27, 1995.

References and Suggested Reading

THERE are numerous lengthy books and countless articles on focus groups. Trade publications, such as *Quirk's Marketing Research Review*, frequently publish articles on focus groups and related types of qualitative research. Below are the books and articles specifically referenced in this book.

Barnhart, Janet. "Focus Group Geography and the Myth of Three Cities." *Alert!*, September 2009.

Craig, Samuel C. and Susan P. Douglas. *International Marketing Research*. Third Edition. New York: John Wiley & Sons, 2005.

Gladwell, Malcolm. *Blink*. New York: Little, Brown and Company, 2005.

Holstein, James A. and Jaber F. Gubrium. *The Active Interview*. Qualitative Research Methods Series 37. Thousand Oaks: Sage, 1995.

McCracken, Grant. *Chief Culture Officer*. New York: Basic Books, 2009.

Rapaille, Clotaire. *The Culture Code*. New York: Broadway Books, 2006.

Schreiber, Theresa and Daryl Gilbert. "International Research: A Phased Approach." *Quirk's Marketing Research Review,* November 2008.

Steel, Jon. *Truth, Lies and Advertising: The Art of Account Planning.* New York: John Wiley and Sons, Inc, 1998.

Sunderland, Patricia L. and Rita M. Denny. *Doing Anthropology in Consumer Research.* Walnut Creek, CA: Left Coast Press, 2007.

Tannen, Deborah. *You're Wearing That?* New York: Random House, 2006.

Weinman, Cynthia. "It's Not Art, But Marketing Research Can Be Creative." *Marketing News,* April 1991.

Zaltman, Gerald. *How Customers Think.* Boston: Harvard Business School Press, 2003.

Index

insights, 9, 93, 111
International Market Research (book), 25
interpretation, 23, 48–49, 71, 101–121
Jonny Lang, 105

Malefyt, Timothy de Waal, 93
McCracken, Grant, 112
memories, 59, 61
moderator
    choosing, 19
    giving direction, 31, 47
    guide for, 31, 93
Mr. Blandings Builds His Dream House (film), 48–49

objectivity, 71, 105
observational research, 7, 9
online research, 27

packaging, 7, 37, 67
purchase intent, 21, 39, 41, 95

Rapaille, Clotaire, 111
Rashomon (film), 71
reporting, 125, 131
research design, 23, 31
responses, meaning of, 116–117

Schreiber, Theresa, 25
Steel, Jon, xvii
strategy, 21
Sunderland, Patricia, xvii, 35

tactics, 21

Tannen, Deborah, 77
techniques
    classification, 53
    collages, 37
    Color Crayon, 37
    deprivation, 57
    diaries, 57, 63
    laddering, 51
    one-on-one, 5
    pairing of brands, 53
    probing, 43
    ZMET, 37
The Active Interview (book), 19
The Culture Code (book), 111
trigger events, 65
Truth, Lies, and Advertising (book), xvii

warm up, xiv, 33
Weinman, Cynthia, 23

You're Wearing That? (book), 77

Zaltman, Gerald, 37

About the author

ROBERT J. MORAIS is a Principal at Weinman Schnee Morais, a marketing research firm located in New York City. Bob has worked for almost 30 years in the advertising and marketing research industries with a wide range of clients. He holds a PhD in anthropology and a certificate from NYU's Stern School of Business. He was a Fulbright Scholar, National Science Foundation Grantee, and Mellon Fellow, and he is a Fellow of The Society for Applied Anthropology. Bob's previous book was *Social Relations in a Philippine Town* and his many scholarly and trade publications encompass anthropology, advertising, and marketing research. He is a frequent guest speaker at industry conferences and business schools.